RIDING WITH INTENT

An Equine Training Journal

Ali Burden-Blake

Riding with Intent - An Equine Training Journal

Copyright © 2018 Alison Burden-Blake. All rights reserved.

Glasgow, Scotland

No parts of this publication may be reproduced, stored in a retrieval system, or transmitted in any form or by any means, electronic, mechanical, photocopying, recording, or otherwise, without the prior written permission of the copyright owner.

This book is sold subject to the condition that it shall not, by way of trade or otherwise, be lent, resold, hired out, or otherwise circulated without the publisher's prior consent in any form of binding or cover other than that in which it is published and without a similar condition including this condition being imposed on the subsequent purchaser. Under no circumstances may any part of this book be photocopied for resale.

RIDING WITH INTENT - *An Equine Training Journal*

HOW TO MAKE THE MOST OF THIS TRAINING JOURNAL

So you picked up this training journal because perhaps you thought "that sounds like a good idea for my horse and I". The thing is though, for it to be useful for you both, you now have to be disciplined, and fill it in everyday. I strongly recommend picking a time of day that works for you, so that filling it in can become a habit, just like your habit of drinking morning coffee! I have always found that, for me, it's sat in bed, just before turning off the lights! I have to make sure that I fill it in the same day, otherwise my sleep seems to have a very effective way of erasing my memory. Whatever works for you!

Keeping track of your schooling sessions, turnout, feed, weather etc. allows you to see where patterns emerge. It also enables you to be more intentional about your riding. This is perhaps one of the most important reasons to keep a journal. You can use it to plan out your week; what days will you school on the flat, jump, hack or lunge. Instead of just getting on and doing what strikes you as a good idea on that day, you'll start to think more about what you need to achieve during each ride. If you walk into the arena with a plan each day it will save you so much time, and that alone will move you closer to your goals much quicker. You will start to weigh up taking an extra day off, with how many sessions you have left before your next event!

"The best preparation for tomorrow is doing your best today." - H. Jackson Brown

Ali Burden-Blake

RIDING WITH INTENT - *An Equine Training Journal*

CONTENTS

How to make the most of this training journal		3
Management Records		
	Horse details	6
	Contacts	7
	Vaccinations	8
	Farrier Visits	8
	Veterinary Visits	9
	Dentist Visits	9
	Saddler Visits	10
	Physiotherapist Visits	10
	Egg Counts	11
	Worming Records	11
	Weight Records	11
Goal Planning		
	Your plan for the year	13
	Where you're currently at	15
	Improvements	16
	Achievements	16
Competition Records		18
Daily Training Records		24

MANAGEMENT RECORDS

HORSE DETAILS

Nickname

Competition Name

Breed

Colour

Height

Age

Sex

Distinctive markings

RIDING WITH INTENT - *An Equine Training Journal*

CONTACTS

	Name	Number
Yard		
Vet		
Farrier		
Dentist		
Saddler		
Physiotherapist		
Feed Merchant		
Instructor		

VACCINATIONS

Vaccine	Due	Given

FARRIER VISITS

Due	Done	Notes

VETERINARY VISITS

Date   Reason   Treatment

DENTIST VISITS

Due   Done   Notes

SADDLER VISITS

Due	Done	Notes

PHYSIO VISITS

Date	Reason	Treatment

EGG COUNTS

Due	Done	Worming Required?

WORMING RECORDS

Due	Done	Wormer Used

WEIGHT RECORDS

Date	Weight	Tape / Scale	Notes

GOAL PLANNING

YOUR PLAN FOR THE YEAR

This is where you map out your shows and aims for the year. If you have other commitments to family and friends, like holiday plans or other events then it's best to start by putting those into the planner first. That way you'll be able to plan your competitive year around them.

Once you have your major shows in place you'll be able to fill in your qualifier shows. Then your training events and lessons.

By doing this you'll start to see a picture of your year ahead, and see where you can take time to introduce new movements or exercises, or give your horse a breather from arena work.

Let's get started!

This pouring thoughts out on paper has relieved me. I feel better and full of confidence and resolution.

Diet Eman

RIDING WITH INTENT - *An Equine Training Journal*

YEAR _____

JANUARY	FEBRUARY	MARCH

APRIL	MAY	JUNE

JULY	AUGUST	SEPTEMBER

OCTOBER	NOVEMBER	DECEMBER

WHERE ARE YOU CURRENTLY AT?

Time to take stock. Where do you feel you're at with your training at the moment? If you get it down on paper then you'll be able to look back at the end of the year and see how far you've come by being organised and diligent with your riding every week.

What was your biggest achievement last year?

What setbacks did you experience last year?

What are your horse's current strengths?

What are your horse's current weaknesses?

IMPROVEMENTS

Now list what improvements you could make through schooling this year

ACHIEVEMENTS

What goals will you have achieved by the 31st of December?

> The power for creating a better future is contained in the present moment: You create a good future by creating a good present.
>
> Eckhart Tolle

COMPETITION RECORDS

COMPETITION RESULTS

Date	Show	Class	Percentage / Faults	Place

COMPETITION RESULTS

Date	Show	Class	Percentage / Faults	Place

COMPETITION RESULTS

Date	Show	Class	Percentage / Faults	Place

COMPETITION RESULTS

Date	Show	Class	Percentage / Faults	Place

There are only two emotions that belong in the saddle; one is a sense of humour and the other is patience.

John Lyons

DAILY TRAINING RECORDS

MONTH: _____

	GOALS / NOTES FOR THE WEEK		
	LUNGED / RIDDEN / HACKED	MANAGEMENT NOTES	
MON ___			WEATHER
			FEED
TUE ___			WEATHER
			FEED
WED ___			WEATHER
			FEED

MONTH: _____

	LUNGED / RIDDEN / HACKED	MANAGEMENT NOTES	
THURS ____			WEATHER
			FEED
FRI ____			WEATHER
			FEED
SAT ____			WEATHER
			FEED
SUN ____			WEATHER
			FEED

MONTH: _____

	LUNGED / RIDDEN / HACKED	MANAGEMENT NOTES	
GOALS / NOTES FOR THE WEEK			
MON _____			WEATHER
			FEED
TUE _____			WEATHER
			FEED
WED _____			WEATHER
			FEED

MONTH: _____

	LUNGED / RIDDEN / HACKED	MANAGEMENT NOTES	
THURS ___			WEATHER
			FEED
FRI ___			WEATHER
			FEED
SAT ___			WEATHER
			FEED
SUN ___			WEATHER
			FEED

There may be people that have more talent than you, but there's no excuse for anyone to work harder than you do.

Derek Jeter

MONTH: _____

	LUNGED / RIDDEN / HACKED	MANAGEMENT NOTES	
GOALS / NOTES FOR THE WEEK			
MON ___			WEATHER
			FEED
TUE ___			WEATHER
			FEED
WED ___			WEATHER
			FEED

MONTH: _____

	LUNGED / RIDDEN / HACKED	MANAGEMENT NOTES	
THURS ___			WEATHER
			FEED
FRI ___			WEATHER
			FEED
SAT ___			WEATHER
			FEED
SUN ___			WEATHER
			FEED

MONTH: _____

	LUNGED / RIDDEN / HACKED	MANAGEMENT NOTES	
GOALS / NOTES FOR THE WEEK			
MON ___			WEATHER
			FEED
TUE ___			WEATHER
			FEED
WED ___			WEATHER
			FEED

MONTH: _____

	LUNGED / RIDDEN / HACKED	MANAGEMENT NOTES	
THURS ___			WEATHER
			FEED
FRI ___			WEATHER
			FEED
SAT ___			WEATHER
			FEED
SUN ___			WEATHER
			FEED

It's not the will to win that matters — everyone has that. It's the will to prepare to win that matters.

Paul "Bear" Bryant

MONTH: _____

GOALS / NOTES FOR THE WEEK			
	LUNGED / RIDDEN / HACKED	MANAGEMENT NOTES	
MON ____			WEATHER
			FEED
TUE ____			WEATHER
			FEED
WED ____			WEATHER
			FEED

MONTH: _____

	LUNGED / RIDDEN / HACKED	MANAGEMENT NOTES	
THURS ____			WEATHER
			FEED
FRI ____			WEATHER
			FEED
SAT ____			WEATHER
			FEED
SUN ____			WEATHER
			FEED

MONTH: _____

	GOALS / NOTES FOR THE WEEK		
	LUNGED / RIDDEN / HACKED	MANAGEMENT NOTES	
MON ___			WEATHER
			FEED
TUE ___			WEATHER
			FEED
WED ___			WEATHER
			FEED

MONTH: _____

	LUNGED / RIDDEN / HACKED	MANAGEMENT NOTES	
THURS ___			WEATHER
			FEED
FRI ___			WEATHER
			FEED
SAT ___			WEATHER
			FEED
SUN ___			WEATHER
			FEED

The principle is competing against yourself. It's about self-improvement, about being better than you were the day before.

Steve Young

MONTH: _____

	GOALS / NOTES FOR THE WEEK		
	LUNGED / RIDDEN / HACKED	MANAGEMENT NOTES	
MON ___			WEATHER
			FEED
TUE ___			WEATHER
			FEED
WED ___			WEATHER
			FEED

MONTH: _____

	LUNGED / RIDDEN / HACKED	MANAGEMENT NOTES	
THURS ___			WEATHER
			FEED
FRI ___			WEATHER
			FEED
SAT ___			WEATHER
			FEED
SUN ___			WEATHER
			FEED

MONTH: _____

	LUNGED / RIDDEN / HACKED	MANAGEMENT NOTES	
GOALS / NOTES FOR THE WEEK			
MON ___			WEATHER
			FEED
TUE ___			WEATHER
			FEED
WED ___			WEATHER
			FEED

MONTH: _____

	LUNGED / RIDDEN / HACKED	MANAGEMENT NOTES		
THURS ____			WEATHER	
			FEED	
FRI ____			WEATHER	
			FEED	
SAT ____			WEATHER	
			FEED	
SUN ____			WEATHER	
			FEED	

MONTH: _____

GOALS / NOTES FOR THE WEEK			
	LUNGED / RIDDEN / HACKED	MANAGEMENT NOTES	
MON ___			WEATHER
			FEED
TUE ___			WEATHER
			FEED
WED ___			WEATHER
			FEED

MONTH: _____

	LUNGED / RIDDEN / HACKED	MANAGEMENT NOTES	
THURS ____			WEATHER
			FEED
FRI ____			WEATHER
			FEED
SAT ____			WEATHER
			FEED
SUN ____			WEATHER
			FEED

MONTH: _____

GOALS / NOTES FOR THE WEEK			
	LUNGED / RIDDEN / HACKED	MANAGEMENT NOTES	
MON ___			WEATHER
			FEED
TUE ___			WEATHER
			FEED
WED ___			WEATHER
			FEED

MONTH: _____

	LUNGED / RIDDEN / HACKED	MANAGEMENT NOTES	
THURS ____			WEATHER
			FEED
FRI ____			WEATHER
			FEED
SAT ____			WEATHER
			FEED
SUN ____			WEATHER
			FEED

The secret in riding is to do only a few things, but to do them right.

Nuno Oliveira

MONTH: _____

	LUNGED / RIDDEN / HACKED	MANAGEMENT NOTES	
GOALS / NOTES FOR THE WEEK			
MON ___			WEATHER
			FEED
TUE ___			WEATHER
			FEED
WED ___			WEATHER
			FEED

MONTH: _____

	LUNGED / RIDDEN / HACKED	MANAGEMENT NOTES	
THURS ____			WEATHER
			FEED
FRI ____			WEATHER
			FEED
SAT ____			WEATHER
			FEED
SUN ____			WEATHER
			FEED

MONTH: _____

	LUNGED / RIDDEN / HACKED	MANAGEMENT NOTES	
GOALS / NOTES FOR THE WEEK			
MON ___			WEATHER
			FEED
TUE ___			WEATHER
			FEED
WED ___			WEATHER
			FEED

MONTH: _____

	LUNGED / RIDDEN / HACKED	MANAGEMENT NOTES	
THURS ____			WEATHER
			FEED
FRI ____			WEATHER
			FEED
SAT ____			WEATHER
			FEED
SUN ____			WEATHER
			FEED

If you really want to do something, you'll find a way. If you don't, you'll find an excuse.

Jim Rohn

MONTH: _____

	LUNGED / RIDDEN / HACKED	MANAGEMENT NOTES	
GOALS / NOTES FOR THE WEEK			
MON ____			WEATHER
			FEED
TUE ____			WEATHER
			FEED
WED ____			WEATHER
			FEED

MONTH: _____

	LUNGED / RIDDEN / HACKED	MANAGEMENT NOTES	
THURS ___			WEATHER
			FEED
FRI ___			WEATHER
			FEED
SAT ___			WEATHER
			FEED
SUN ___			WEATHER
			FEED

MONTH: _____

	LUNGED / RIDDEN / HACKED	MANAGEMENT NOTES	
GOALS / NOTES FOR THE WEEK			
MON ___			WEATHER
			FEED
TUE ___			WEATHER
			FEED
WED ___			WEATHER
			FEED

MONTH: _____

	LUNGED / RIDDEN / HACKED	MANAGEMENT NOTES	
THURS ____			WEATHER
			FEED
FRI ____			WEATHER
			FEED
SAT ____			WEATHER
			FEED
SUN ____			WEATHER
			FEED

Fall seven times and stand up eight.

Japanese Proverb

MONTH: _____

	LUNGED / RIDDEN / HACKED	MANAGEMENT NOTES	
GOALS / NOTES FOR THE WEEK			
MON ____			WEATHER
			FEED
TUE ____			WEATHER
			FEED
WED ____			WEATHER
			FEED

MONTH: _____

	LUNGED / RIDDEN / HACKED	MANAGEMENT NOTES	
THURS ___			WEATHER
			FEED
FRI ___			WEATHER
			FEED
SAT ___			WEATHER
			FEED
SUN ___			WEATHER
			FEED

MONTH: _____

	GOALS / NOTES FOR THE WEEK		
	LUNGED / RIDDEN / HACKED	MANAGEMENT NOTES	
MON ___			WEATHER
			FEED
TUE ___			WEATHER
			FEED
WED ___			WEATHER
			FEED

MONTH: _____

	LUNGED / RIDDEN / HACKED	MANAGEMENT NOTES	
THURS ___			WEATHER
			FEED
FRI ___			WEATHER
			FEED
SAT ___			WEATHER
			FEED
SUN ___			WEATHER
			FEED

In order to succeed, we must first believe that we can.

Nikos Kazantzakis

MONTH: _____

GOALS / NOTES FOR THE WEEK			
	LUNGED / RIDDEN / HACKED	MANAGEMENT NOTES	
MON ____			WEATHER
			FEED
TUE ____			WEATHER
			FEED
WED ____			WEATHER
			FEED

MONTH: _____

	LUNGED / RIDDEN / HACKED	MANAGEMENT NOTES	
THURS ___			WEATHER
			FEED
FRI ___			WEATHER
			FEED
SAT ___			WEATHER
			FEED
SUN ___			WEATHER
			FEED

MONTH: _____

GOALS / NOTES FOR THE WEEK			
	LUNGED / RIDDEN / HACKED	MANAGEMENT NOTES	
MON _____			WEATHER
			FEED
TUE _____			WEATHER
			FEED
WED _____			WEATHER
			FEED

MONTH: _____

	LUNGED / RIDDEN / HACKED	MANAGEMENT NOTES	
THURS ___			WEATHER
			FEED
FRI ___			WEATHER
			FEED
SAT ___			WEATHER
			FEED
SUN ___			WEATHER
			FEED

Just keep going. Everybody gets better if they keep at it.

Ted Williams

MONTH: _____

	GOALS / NOTES FOR THE WEEK		
	LUNGED / RIDDEN / HACKED	MANAGEMENT NOTES	
MON ____			WEATHER
			FEED
TUE ____			WEATHER
			FEED
WED ____			WEATHER
			FEED

MONTH: _____

	LUNGED / RIDDEN / HACKED	MANAGEMENT NOTES	
THURS ____			WEATHER
			FEED
FRI ____			WEATHER
			FEED
SAT ____			WEATHER
			FEED
SUN ____			WEATHER
			FEED

MONTH: _____

	GOALS / NOTES FOR THE WEEK		
	LUNGED / RIDDEN / HACKED	MANAGEMENT NOTES	
MON ____			WEATHER
			FEED
TUE ____			WEATHER
			FEED
WED ____			WEATHER
			FEED

MONTH: _____

	LUNGED / RIDDEN / HACKED	MANAGEMENT NOTES	
THURS ___			WEATHER
			FEED
FRI ___			WEATHER
			FEED
SAT ___			WEATHER
			FEED
SUN ___			WEATHER
			FEED

When you want something, all the universe conspires in helping you to achieve it.

The Alchemist

MONTH: _____

	LUNGED / RIDDEN / HACKED	MANAGEMENT NOTES	
GOALS / NOTES FOR THE WEEK			
MON ____			WEATHER
			FEED
TUE ____			WEATHER
			FEED
WED ____			WEATHER
			FEED

MONTH: _____

	LUNGED / RIDDEN / HACKED	MANAGEMENT NOTES	
THURS ___			WEATHER
			FEED
FRI ___			WEATHER
			FEED
SAT ___			WEATHER
			FEED
SUN ___			WEATHER
			FEED

MONTH: _____

	LUNGED / RIDDEN / HACKED	MANAGEMENT NOTES	
GOALS / NOTES FOR THE WEEK			
MON ____			WEATHER
			FEED
TUE ____			WEATHER
			FEED
WED ____			WEATHER
			FEED

MONTH: _____

	LUNGED / RIDDEN / HACKED	MANAGEMENT NOTES	
THURS ____			WEATHER
			FEED
FRI ____			WEATHER
			FEED
SAT ____			WEATHER
			FEED
SUN ____			WEATHER
			FEED

Do or do not, there is no 'try'.

Yoda

MONTH: _____

	LUNGED / RIDDEN / HACKED	MANAGEMENT NOTES	
GOALS / NOTES FOR THE WEEK			
MON ___			WEATHER
			FEED
TUE ___			WEATHER
			FEED
WED ___			WEATHER
			FEED

MONTH: _____

	LUNGED / RIDDEN / HACKED	MANAGEMENT NOTES	
THURS ___			WEATHER
			FEED
FRI ___			WEATHER
			FEED
SAT ___			WEATHER
			FEED
SUN ___			WEATHER
			FEED

MONTH: _____

	GOALS / NOTES FOR THE WEEK		
	LUNGED / RIDDEN / HACKED	MANAGEMENT NOTES	
MON ____			WEATHER
			FEED
TUE ____			WEATHER
			FEED
WED ____			WEATHER
			FEED

MONTH: _____

	LUNGED / RIDDEN / HACKED	MANAGEMENT NOTES	
THURS ____			WEATHER
			FEED
FRI ____			WEATHER
			FEED
SAT ____			WEATHER
			FEED
SUN ____			WEATHER
			FEED

What are the three things you must have in order to become a good rider?

1. A good seat.
2. A good seat.
3. A good seat.

Jack Le Goff

MONTH: _____

	GOALS / NOTES FOR THE WEEK		
	LUNGED / RIDDEN / HACKED	MANAGEMENT NOTES	
MON ___			WEATHER
			FEED
TUE ___			WEATHER
			FEED
WED ___			WEATHER
			FEED

MONTH: _____

	LUNGED / RIDDEN / HACKED	MANAGEMENT NOTES	
THURS ___			WEATHER
			FEED
FRI ___			WEATHER
			FEED
SAT ___			WEATHER
			FEED
SUN ___			WEATHER
			FEED

MONTH: _____

	GOALS / NOTES FOR THE WEEK		
	LUNGED / RIDDEN / HACKED	MANAGEMENT NOTES	
MON ____			WEATHER
			FEED
TUE ____			WEATHER
			FEED
WED ____			WEATHER
			FEED

MONTH: _____

	LUNGED / RIDDEN / HACKED	MANAGEMENT NOTES	
THURS ___			WEATHER
			FEED
FRI ___			WEATHER
			FEED
SAT ___			WEATHER
			FEED
SUN ___			WEATHER
			FEED

All top riders have mastered the ability to be in the moment and stay mindful during their ride. It is also, thankfully, something you can successfully enhance no matter what your level of physical expertise.

Tonya Johnston

MONTH: _____

	GOALS / NOTES FOR THE WEEK		
	LUNGED / RIDDEN / HACKED	MANAGEMENT NOTES	
MON ___			WEATHER
			FEED
TUE ___			WEATHER
			FEED
WED ___			WEATHER
			FEED

MONTH: _____

	LUNGED / RIDDEN / HACKED	MANAGEMENT NOTES	
THURS ____			WEATHER
			FEED
FRI ____			WEATHER
			FEED
SAT ____			WEATHER
			FEED
SUN ____			WEATHER
			FEED

MONTH: _____

	LUNGED / RIDDEN / HACKED	MANAGEMENT NOTES	
GOALS / NOTES FOR THE WEEK			
MON ___			WEATHER
			FEED
TUE ___			WEATHER
			FEED
WED ___			WEATHER
			FEED

MONTH: _____

	LUNGED / RIDDEN / HACKED	MANAGEMENT NOTES	
THURS ___			WEATHER
			FEED
FRI ___			WEATHER
			FEED
SAT ___			WEATHER
			FEED
SUN ___			WEATHER
			FEED

*Horse-training is details.
Little details.*

George Morris

MONTH: _____

	LUNGED / RIDDEN / HACKED	MANAGEMENT NOTES	
GOALS / NOTES FOR THE WEEK			
MON ___			WEATHER
			FEED
TUE ___			WEATHER
			FEED
WED ___			WEATHER
			FEED

MONTH: _____

	LUNGED / RIDDEN / HACKED	MANAGEMENT NOTES	
THURS _____			WEATHER
			FEED
FRI _____			WEATHER
			FEED
SAT _____			WEATHER
			FEED
SUN _____			WEATHER
			FEED

MONTH: _____

	GOALS / NOTES FOR THE WEEK		
	LUNGED / RIDDEN / HACKED	MANAGEMENT NOTES	
MON ___			WEATHER
			FEED
TUE ___			WEATHER
			FEED
WED ___			WEATHER
			FEED

MONTH: _____

	LUNGED / RIDDEN / HACKED	MANAGEMENT NOTES	
THURS ___			WEATHER
			FEED
FRI ___			WEATHER
			FEED
SAT ___			WEATHER
			FEED
SUN ___			WEATHER
			FEED

We all get so excited about the big events, but when there's an animal involved, it's ten times harder.

Charlotte Dujardin

MONTH: _____

GOALS / NOTES FOR THE WEEK			
	LUNGED / RIDDEN / HACKED	MANAGEMENT NOTES	
MON ___			WEATHER
			FEED
TUE ___			WEATHER
			FEED
WED ___			WEATHER
			FEED

MONTH: _____

	LUNGED / RIDDEN / HACKED	MANAGEMENT NOTES	
THURS ____			WEATHER
			FEED
FRI ____			WEATHER
			FEED
SAT ____			WEATHER
			FEED
SUN ____			WEATHER
			FEED

MONTH: _____

	GOALS / NOTES FOR THE WEEK		
	LUNGED / RIDDEN / HACKED	MANAGEMENT NOTES	
MON ___			WEATHER
			FEED
TUE ___			WEATHER
			FEED
WED ___			WEATHER
			FEED

MONTH: _____

	LUNGED / RIDDEN / HACKED	MANAGEMENT NOTES	
THURS			WEATHER
			FEED
FRI ___			WEATHER
			FEED
SAT ___			WEATHER
			FEED
SUN ___			WEATHER
			FEED

In the end, we don't know what horses can do. We only know that when, over the past thousands of years, we have asked something more of them, at least some of them have readily supplied it.

Jane Smiley

MONTH: _____

	GOALS / NOTES FOR THE WEEK		
	LUNGED / RIDDEN / HACKED	MANAGEMENT NOTES	
MON ___			WEATHER
			FEED
TUE ___			WEATHER
			FEED
WED ___			WEATHER
			FEED

MONTH: _____

	LUNGED / RIDDEN / HACKED	MANAGEMENT NOTES	
THURS ____			WEATHER
			FEED
FRI ____			WEATHER
			FEED
SAT ____			WEATHER
			FEED
SUN ____			WEATHER
			FEED

MONTH: _____

	GOALS / NOTES FOR THE WEEK		
	LUNGED / RIDDEN / HACKED	MANAGEMENT NOTES	
MON ____			WEATHER
			FEED
TUE ____			WEATHER
			FEED
WED ____			WEATHER
			FEED

MONTH: _____

	LUNGED / RIDDEN / HACKED	MANAGEMENT NOTES	
THURS ____			WEATHER FEED
FRI ____			WEATHER FEED
SAT ____			WEATHER FEED
SUN ____			WEATHER FEED

A horse gallops with his lungs, perseveres with his heart, and wins with his character.

                                              Tesio

MONTH: _____

GOALS / NOTES FOR THE WEEK			
	LUNGED / RIDDEN / HACKED	**MANAGEMENT NOTES**	
MON ___			**WEATHER**
			FEED
TUE ___			**WEATHER**
			FEED
WED ___			**WEATHER**
			FEED

MONTH: _____

	LUNGED / RIDDEN / HACKED	MANAGEMENT NOTES	
THURS ____			WEATHER
			FEED
FRI ____			WEATHER
			FEED
SAT ____			WEATHER
			FEED
SUN ____			WEATHER
			FEED

MONTH: _____

GOALS / NOTES FOR THE WEEK			
	LUNGED / RIDDEN / HACKED	MANAGEMENT NOTES	
MON ____			WEATHER
			FEED
TUE ____			WEATHER
			FEED
WED ____			WEATHER
			FEED

MONTH: _____

	LUNGED / RIDDEN / HACKED	MANAGEMENT NOTES	
THURS ____			WEATHER
			FEED
FRI ____			WEATHER
			FEED
SAT ____			WEATHER
			FEED
SUN ____			WEATHER
			FEED

Success is not the key to happiness. Happiness is the key to success. If you love what you are doing, you will be successful.

Albert Schweitzer

MONTH: _____

	GOALS / NOTES FOR THE WEEK		
	LUNGED / RIDDEN / HACKED	MANAGEMENT NOTES	
MON ___			WEATHER
			FEED
TUE ___			WEATHER
			FEED
WED ___			WEATHER
			FEED

MONTH: _____

	LUNGED / RIDDEN / HACKED	MANAGEMENT NOTES	
THURS ___			WEATHER
			FEED
FRI ___			WEATHER
			FEED
SAT ___			WEATHER
			FEED
SUN ___			WEATHER
			FEED

MONTH: _____

GOALS / NOTES FOR THE WEEK			
	LUNGED / RIDDEN / HACKED	**MANAGEMENT NOTES**	
MON ___			**WEATHER**
			FEED
TUE ___			**WEATHER**
			FEED
WED ___			**WEATHER**
			FEED

MONTH: _____

	LUNGED / RIDDEN / HACKED	MANAGEMENT NOTES	
THURS ____			WEATHER
			FEED
FRI ____			WEATHER
			FEED
SAT ____			WEATHER
			FEED
SUN ____			WEATHER
			FEED

*In riding a horse,
we borrow freedom.*

                                                Helen Thompson

MONTH:_____

	LUNGED / RIDDEN / HACKED	MANAGEMENT NOTES	
GOALS / NOTES FOR THE WEEK			
MON ____			WEATHER
			FEED
TUE ____			WEATHER
			FEED
WED ____			WEATHER
			FEED

MONTH: _____

	LUNGED / RIDDEN / HACKED	MANAGEMENT NOTES	
THURS ____			WEATHER
			FEED
FRI ____			WEATHER
			FEED
SAT ____			WEATHER
			FEED
SUN ____			WEATHER
			FEED

MONTH: _____

	LUNGED / RIDDEN / HACKED	MANAGEMENT NOTES	
GOALS / NOTES FOR THE WEEK			
MON _____			WEATHER
			FEED
TUE _____			WEATHER
			FEED
WED _____			WEATHER
			FEED

MONTH: _____

	LUNGED / RIDDEN / HACKED	MANAGEMENT NOTES	
THURS ____			WEATHER
			FEED
FRI ____			WEATHER
			FEED
SAT ____			WEATHER
			FEED
SUN ____			WEATHER
			FEED

Keep away from people who try to belittle your ambitions. Small people always do that, but the really great make you feel that you, too, can become great.

Mark Twain

MONTH: _____

	GOALS / NOTES FOR THE WEEK		
	LUNGED / RIDDEN / HACKED	MANAGEMENT NOTES	
MON ____			WEATHER
			FEED
TUE ____			WEATHER
			FEED
WED ____			WEATHER
			FEED

MONTH: _____

	LUNGED / RIDDEN / HACKED	MANAGEMENT NOTES	
THURS ___			WEATHER
			FEED
FRI ___			WEATHER
			FEED
SAT ___			WEATHER
			FEED
SUN ___			WEATHER
			FEED

MONTH: _____

GOALS / NOTES FOR THE WEEK			
	LUNGED / RIDDEN / HACKED	MANAGEMENT NOTES	
MON ___			WEATHER
			FEED
TUE ___			WEATHER
			FEED
WED ___			WEATHER
			FEED

MONTH: _____

	LUNGED / RIDDEN / HACKED	MANAGEMENT NOTES	
THURS ___			WEATHER
			FEED
FRI ___			WEATHER
			FEED
SAT ___			WEATHER
			FEED
SUN ___			WEATHER
			FEED

Follow your passion. Stay true to yourself. Never follow someone else's path unless you're in the woods and you're lost and you see a path. By all means, you should follow that.

Ellen DeGeneres

MONTH: _____

	LUNGED / RIDDEN / HACKED	MANAGEMENT NOTES	
GOALS / NOTES FOR THE WEEK			
MON _____			WEATHER
			FEED
TUE _____			WEATHER
			FEED
WED _____			WEATHER
			FEED

MONTH: _____

	LUNGED / RIDDEN / HACKED	MANAGEMENT NOTES	
THURS ____			WEATHER
			FEED
FRI ____			WEATHER
			FEED
SAT ____			WEATHER
			FEED
SUN ____			WEATHER
			FEED

MONTH: _____

	LUNGED / RIDDEN / HACKED	MANAGEMENT NOTES	
GOALS / NOTES FOR THE WEEK			
MON _____			WEATHER
			FEED
TUE _____			WEATHER
			FEED
WED _____			WEATHER
			FEED

MONTH: _____

	LUNGED / RIDDEN / HACKED	MANAGEMENT NOTES	
THURS ___			WEATHER
			FEED
FRI ___			WEATHER
			FEED
SAT ___			WEATHER
			FEED
SUN ___			WEATHER
			FEED

You miss 100% of the shots you don't take.

Wayne Gretzky

MONTH: _____

	GOALS / NOTES FOR THE WEEK		
	LUNGED / RIDDEN / HACKED	MANAGEMENT NOTES	
MON ___			WEATHER
			FEED
TUE ___			WEATHER
			FEED
WED ___			WEATHER
			FEED

MONTH: _____

	LUNGED / RIDDEN / HACKED	MANAGEMENT NOTES	
THURS ___			WEATHER
			FEED
FRI ___			WEATHER
			FEED
SAT ___			WEATHER
			FEED
SUN ___			WEATHER
			FEED

MONTH: _____

	GOALS / NOTES FOR THE WEEK		
	LUNGED / RIDDEN / HACKED	MANAGEMENT NOTES	
MON ___			WEATHER
			FEED
TUE ___			WEATHER
			FEED
WED ___			WEATHER
			FEED

MONTH: _____

	LUNGED / RIDDEN / HACKED	MANAGEMENT NOTES	
THURS ____			WEATHER
			FEED
FRI ____			WEATHER
			FEED
SAT ____			WEATHER
			FEED
SUN ____			WEATHER
			FEED

Practice isn't the thing you do once you're good. It's the thing you do that makes you good.

Malcolm Gladwell

MONTH: _____

	LUNGED / RIDDEN / HACKED	MANAGEMENT NOTES	
GOALS / NOTES FOR THE WEEK			
MON ___			WEATHER
			FEED
TUE ___			WEATHER
			FEED
WED ___			WEATHER
			FEED

MONTH: _____

	LUNGED / RIDDEN / HACKED	MANAGEMENT NOTES	
THURS ___			WEATHER
			FEED
FRI ___			WEATHER
			FEED
SAT ___			WEATHER
			FEED
SUN ___			WEATHER
			FEED

MONTH: _____

	LUNGED / RIDDEN / HACKED	MANAGEMENT NOTES	
GOALS / NOTES FOR THE WEEK			
MON ____			WEATHER
			FEED
TUE ____			WEATHER
			FEED
WED ____			WEATHER
			FEED

MONTH: _____

	LUNGED / RIDDEN / HACKED	MANAGEMENT NOTES	
THURS ___			WEATHER
			FEED
FRI ___			WEATHER
			FEED
SAT ___			WEATHER
			FEED
SUN ___			WEATHER
			FEED

Sports do not build character. They reveal it.

                                                      Heywood Broun

MONTH: _____

	GOALS / NOTES FOR THE WEEK		
	LUNGED / RIDDEN / HACKED	MANAGEMENT NOTES	
MON ___			WEATHER
			FEED
TUE ___			WEATHER
			FEED
WED ___			WEATHER
			FEED

MONTH: _____

	LUNGED / RIDDEN / HACKED	MANAGEMENT NOTES	
THURS _____			WEATHER
			FEED
FRI _____			WEATHER
			FEED
SAT _____			WEATHER
			FEED
SUN _____			WEATHER
			FEED

MONTH: _____

GOALS / NOTES FOR THE WEEK			
	LUNGED / RIDDEN / HACKED	MANAGEMENT NOTES	
MON ___			WEATHER
			FEED
TUE ___			WEATHER
			FEED
WED ___			WEATHER
			FEED

MONTH: _____

	LUNGED / RIDDEN / HACKED	MANAGEMENT NOTES	
THURS ___			WEATHER
			FEED
FRI ___			WEATHER
			FEED
SAT ___			WEATHER
			FEED
SUN ___			WEATHER
			FEED

After 10 strides, the horse knows if he is the leader or if his rider is the leader.

Kyra Kyrklund

MONTH: _____

	LUNGED / RIDDEN / HACKED	MANAGEMENT NOTES	
GOALS / NOTES FOR THE WEEK			
MON ___			WEATHER
			FEED
TUE ___			WEATHER
			FEED
WED ___			WEATHER
			FEED

MONTH: _____

	LUNGED / RIDDEN / HACKED	MANAGEMENT NOTES	
THURS ___			WEATHER
			FEED
FRI ___			WEATHER
			FEED
SAT ___			WEATHER
			FEED
SUN ___			WEATHER
			FEED

MONTH: _____

	LUNGED / RIDDEN / HACKED	MANAGEMENT NOTES	
GOALS / NOTES FOR THE WEEK			
MON ___			WEATHER
			FEED
TUE ___			WEATHER
			FEED
WED ___			WEATHER
			FEED

MONTH: _____

	LUNGED / RIDDEN / HACKED	MANAGEMENT NOTES	
THURS ___			WEATHER
			FEED
FRI ___			WEATHER
			FEED
SAT ___			WEATHER
			FEED
SUN ___			WEATHER
			FEED

It seemed to us there was no other outcome than we'd win. We just didn't believe it could go wrong.

Ben Maher, on the team at London Olympics 2012

MONTH: _____

	GOALS / NOTES FOR THE WEEK		

	LUNGED / RIDDEN / HACKED	MANAGEMENT NOTES	
MON ____			WEATHER
			FEED
TUE ____			WEATHER
			FEED
WED ____			WEATHER
			FEED

MONTH: _____

	LUNGED / RIDDEN / HACKED	MANAGEMENT NOTES	
THURS _____			WEATHER
			FEED
FRI _____			WEATHER
			FEED
SAT _____			WEATHER
			FEED
SUN _____			WEATHER
			FEED

MONTH: _____

	LUNGED / RIDDEN / HACKED	MANAGEMENT NOTES	
GOALS / NOTES FOR THE WEEK			
MON ___			WEATHER
			FEED
TUE ___			WEATHER
			FEED
WED ___			WEATHER
			FEED

MONTH: _____

	LUNGED / RIDDEN / HACKED	MANAGEMENT NOTES	
THURS ___			WEATHER
			FEED
FRI ___			WEATHER
			FEED
SAT ___			WEATHER
			FEED
SUN ___			WEATHER
			FEED

When it rains, look for rainbows, when it's dark, look for stars.

Made in the USA
Middletown, DE
14 November 2020